TWISTY TALES

The Magic Pudding Pot

by Kay Woodward

and Sheena Dempsey

W

FRANKLIN WATTS

LONDON•SYDNEY

This story is based on the traditional fairy tale,
The Magic Porridge Pot, but with a new twist.
You can read the original story in
Must Know Stories. Can you make
up your own twist for the story?

Franklin Watts
First published in Great Britain in 2016
by the Watts Publishing Group

Copyright (text) © Kay Woodward 2016
Copyright (illustrations) © Sheena Dempsey 2016

The rights of Kay Woodward to be identified as the
author and Sheena Dempsey as the illustrator of this Work have been
asserted in accordance with the Copyright, Designs and
Patents Act, 1988.

ISBN 978 1 4451 4791 8 (hbk)
ISBN 978 1 4451 4793 2 (pbk)
ISBN 978 1 4451 4792 5 (library ebook)

Series Editor: Melanie Palmer
Series Advisor: Catherine Glavina
Series Designer: Peter Scoulding
Cover Designer: Cathryn Gilbert

Printed in China

Franklin Watts
An imprint of
Hachette Children's Group
Part of The Watts Publishing Group
Carmelite House
50 Victoria Embankment
London EC4Y 0DZ

An Hachette UK Company
www.hachette.co.uk

www.franklinwatts.co.uk

MIX
Paper from
responsible sources

FSC
www.fsc.org
FSC® C104740

Once upon a time, there lived a
girl and her mother who ate
nothing but vegetables.

The mother loved vegetables.
The girl did not.
"I never want to see another
piece of broccoli!" she sobbed.

"But it's so good for you!" said her mother. "Here, have some more."

Then, one day, the saucepan
snapped in two.

"Oh dear," said her mother.

She sent the girl to the
supermarket to buy a new one.

The girl looked at the shiny
new saucepans.

"If I buy one of those," she
thought, "I'll have to eat EVEN
MORE vegetables."

Then she spotted a tiny golden pot.

POTS

COOK YOUR
FAVOURITE
FOOD,
EVERY DAY

Beside the tiny golden pot there was an even tinier sign. "Cook your favourite food every day," it read.

COOK YOUR
FAVOURITE
FOOD,
EVERY DAY

"No more vegetables!" sang the girl. She paid for the cooking pot, put it under her arm and danced all the way home.

At home, the girl read the instructions:

Tell the cooking pot what to cook and say, "Cook, little pot, cook."
To stop cooking, say, "Stop, little pot, stop."

"Sticky toffee pudding!" said the girl. "Cook, little pot, cook." The cooking pot blipped and blopped and bibbled and bubbled.

When the girl lifted the lid,
there was a sticky toffee
pudding inside.
"Stop, little pot, stop," she said.

It was delicious. Even her mother liked it. (Though she wished there had been carrots and cauliflower too.)

"Creamy rice pudding!" said the girl, the next day. "Cook, little pot, cook." The cooking pot blipped and blopped and bibbled and bubbled until the girl said, "Stop, little pot, stop."

Inside, there was a creamy rice pudding. They ate it all up. (Though her mother missed peppers and potatoes.)

Every day, the girl asked for a new pudding. The cooking pot made apple pie, vanilla cheesecake and strawberry jelly.

It made ice cream, lemon tart and banana split. (By now, the girl's mother longed for salad.)

One day, the girl asked for chocolate pudding. Then she went for a sleep because she was so full of pudding.

The cooking pot boiled and bubbled. And because no one told it to stop, it went on cooking.

Soon, chocolate pudding filled the kitchen. It filled the house.

And then it poured out of the house into the town.

By teatime, the town was
sitting in a chocolate
pudding lake.

Mutts' Cuts

CROCKS

"Oh no! What shall we do?" cried the mother. The girl awoke. "Oops," she said. "Stop, little pot." The cooking pot stopped cooking at last.

The girl dipped her finger into the chocolate pudding. She licked it. "I'm bored of pudding," she said.

"Fresh vegetables for tea?"
said her mother.
The girl smiled.
"Yes, PLEASE!"

Puzzle 1

Put these pictures in the correct order.
Which event do you think is most important?
Now try writing the story in your own words!

Puzzle 2

1. I am very sleepy.

2. I like being healthy.

3. I love chocolate!

4. I hate eating broccoli.

5. The more greens the better!

6. You can't have enough vegetables!

Choose the correct speech bubbles for each character. Can you think of any others? Turn over to find the answers.

Answers

Puzzle 1

The correct order is: 1f, 2b, 3c, 4a, 5e, 6d

Puzzle 2

Girl: 1, 3, 4

Mum: 2, 5, 6

Look out for more Hopscotch Twisty Tales

The Ninjabread Man
ISBN 978 1 4451 3964 7
The Boy Who Cried Sheep!
ISBN 978 1 4451 4292 0
Thumbelina Thinks Big
ISBN 978 1 4451 4295 1
**Move versus the
Enormous Turnip**
ISBN 978 1 4451 4300 2
Big Pancacke to the Rescue
ISBN 978 1 4451 4303 3
Little Red Hen's Great Escape
ISBN 978 1 4451 4305 7
The Lovely Duckling
ISBN 978 1 4451 1633 4
**Hansel and Gretel
and the Green Witch**
ISBN 978 1 4451 1634 1
The Emperor's New Kit
ISBN 978 1 4451 1635 8

**Rapunzel and the
Prince of Pop**
ISBN 978 1 4451 1636 5
**Dick Whittington
Gets on his Bike**
ISBN 978 1 4451 1637 2
**The Pied Piper and
the Wrong Song**
ISBN 978 1 4451 1638 9
**The Princess and the
Frozen Peas**
ISBN 978 1 4451 0675 5
Snow White Sees the Light
ISBN 978 1 4451 0676 2
**The Elves and the
Trendy Shoes**
ISBN 978 1 4451 0678 6
The Three Frilly Goats Fluff
ISBN 978 1 4451 0677 9

Princess Frog
ISBN 978 1 4451 0679 3
Rumpled Stilton Skin
ISBN 978 1 4451 0680 9
Jack and the Bean Pie
ISBN 978 1 4451 0182 8
**Brownilocks and the Three Bowl
of Cornflakes**
ISBN 978 1 4451 0183 5
Cinderella's Big Foot
ISBN 978 1 4451 0184 2
Little Bad Riding Hood
ISBN 978 1 4451 0185 9
**Sleeping Beauty –
100 Years Later**
ISBN 978 1 4451 0186 6
**The Three Little Pigs &
the New Neighbour**
ISBN 978 1 4451 0181 1

For more Hopscotch books go to:
www.franklinwatts.co.uk